Healthy Smoothie Diet

Become An Expert In A Short Time Harry L. Foster

Harry L. Foster

Contents

Chapter 1

Introduction

Healthy Smoothie Diet_

Become An Expert In A Short Time

Author

Harry L. Foster

FOREWORD

I had some actual Indeedbeing worries before I began eating according to my blood categorization. I was diagnosed with joint pain in my mid-40s, so I was used to throbs in my neck and the occasional throb in my hip, but only lately have I noticed serious problems. To get into a car, I had to raise my leg with my hand since my thigh muscles were so fragile.

My knees felt so badly that I couldn't sleep in the evenings. Then there were the nights when my shins, calves, and/or toes were squeezing excessively. I'd walk the virus tile floor seeking relief as the discomfort brought tears to my eyes. Given my age, I assumed these were typical "old lady" concerns as I approached 60. When my partner started researching eating food kinds compatible with one's blood type, I was about to go to a professional for a resolution to the problem. I opted to check out the eating regimen before seeking clinical therapy since I don't "do doctoring." So far, the eating regimen has had a noticeable impact. I've observed a nearly 90% improvement in my thigh muscles in only 90 days of following the food plan, and my night knee pains are vanished.

Alcohol, which works as a poison in my system, is to blame for the occasional wakeful evenings with cramps and headaches. I didn't realize that drinking more than one glass of wine on a daily basis could have such a bad effect on me since I never drank more than one on a regular basis. However, according to D'Adamo, Os are unable to consume alcoholic beverages. That helped me figure out what was causing my nighttime cramps, and I began to pay attention to when they occurred. When we had visitors or went out to dinner, and I drank more than one glass of wine, I recognized it. There are some fantastic-tasting cocktails, and I'm known for preparing a mean "fun drink," generally with Baileys or Kailua; Margaritas, Chi Chis, and so on, and just one would never be enough. I would experience cramps at those occasions. When I go out now, I make a conscious effort to limit myself to one drink. Who'd have guessed that the answer to my problems would be so straightforward? It was just a matter of changing my eating habits that I was able to achieve my goals.

Cooking has always been a passion of mine since I was in elementary school, about 40 years ago (e-strays). When I decided to transfer to Michigan State University in East Lansing, Michigan, I was attending a small kids' school focused on retail marketing.

The School of Business and the School of Home Economics each have their own retail program at Michigan State. The two schools had similar needs, thus the offices were combined for a long period. The classrooms, however, were distinct. Foods & Nutrition, Child Care, and Child Psychology were all given by the Home Economics Department. I believed it was a good opportunity to learn about cooking while also learning about child brain research and development, because I wanted six children and my mother had never let me into the kitchen.

My first marriage after college provided me with the opportunity to cook breakfast, noon, and dinner. My first experience with a gas oven will be with me forever. I ended up with burned hair and burnt eyelashes after never using a pilot light.

My intentions, on the other hand, were not exactly like those in the books at any time. I was tinkering with a little bit of this and a little bit of that the whole time. My family never had any pre-packaged cakes, sweets, or freezer dinners since I enjoyed cooking so much. They didn't view this as an advantage, obviously.

Until we moved to Los Angeles, California in 1970, I was content with my Bible-based cookbooks. I became quite aware of the exhaust cloud and got involved in the natural evolution very fast. My old worn out, food stained volumes of scriptures were replaced with Adelle Davis' Let's Cook It Right and other wellness food cookbooks. I had three children at the time, and our grocery shopping routine included a trip to the egg ranch for free-range eggs and a trip to the dairy for raw milk and cheddar cheese. Food substitutes were commonplace back then. White flour, white bread, white sugar, and salt were no longer acceptable. Whole wheat flour, raw grain in everything, whole wheat, nut, and multi grain breads, honey, and cinnamon and nutmeg bunches were in its place. The nursery was bursting with tomatoes, green peppers, zucchinis, strawberries, apricot, orange, and lemon trees, and our kitchen was stocked with huge containers of seeds and nuts. Each evening, the older kids came home from school to frozen yogurt shakes made with powdered milk, brewer's yeast, and new natural items; their popsicles were made with handcrafted yogurt; and their friends were welcomed to carrot and celery sticks dipped in peanut butter. I've been the narrator of a few of their favorite childhood tales up until now. They are always reminding me of their peanut butter, cheddar, lettuce, and jam sandwiches.

They complained that they seldom saw anybody at school with whom they might trade lunches, thus the sandwiches usually ended up in the garbage. When my two youngest children were born, I was completely obsessed with protecting them from toxins and synthetic substances in food. No kid food or nutrition was ever given to the newborns. They ate everything we ate, but it was pureed in the blender for them.

For the next 20 years, the eating habits remained virtually unchanged until tragedy struck the family when my oldest kid died. After that, I changed my eating habits. I went from being a lacto-vegetarian to being lacto-vegetarian. Mysticism taught me to value each creature's daily routine. I'd consume a monster's side effects, but not the thing itself. I ate a lot of whole grains, new natural goods, veggies, nuts, cheeses, eggs, milk, yogurt, and diet cola for dinner. One drawback was a once-a-month chewing urge, which made me want red meat. We'd go to the meat market for a steak or a steakhouse for a delicious rib supper during those times.

We were visiting a friend's mountain property some years ago, and I obtained a copy of Dr. D'Adamo's book Eat Right For Your Type from them. I found it fascinating to read and speculated that he and his father could be onto something important in terms of nutrition. It was especially noticeable that red meat is beneficial to Os. Maybe that's why I craved steak or prime rib every now and then, I reasoned at the time.

A friend had begun to educate me on her new dietary routine two months previously. As I read the book, my ears pricked up. I rushed to the bookstore and purchased a copy of Eat Right For Your Type, which I devoured late into the night. I bought the cookbook the next day, but it wasn't quite what I was looking for. I wanted a cookbook that focused only on the O blood type's BENEFICIAL* food types. I started madly reproducing my ideas after 20 years. As I've resumed eating meat and fish, I've started making the sign of the cross and offering thankfulness to the animals.

As I put these ideas together for myself, it occurred to me that each blood type might benefit from a cookbook of this kind.

BLOOD TYPE O Arthritis/Joint Inflammation, Blood Disorders, Stroke? BLOOD TYPE O Arthritis/Joint Inflammation, Blood Disorders, Stroke?

Chapter 2

HOW TO MAKE PROFITABLE RECIPES

THERE IS A REASON WHY WE GET SICK AND FAT, OR WHY WE STAY HEALTHY AND VIBRANT!

The original blood type was thought to be O, and meat was the primary source of protein. However, since man had to relocate to other places where meat was scarce or unavailable, he had to adjust his dietary habits to survive. The other three blood classes gained ground as a result of change. Type A blood types adapted quickly to a vegan diet, and when additional food sources were available, man adapted to the stockpile once more, resulting in the B and AB blood types.

As a result of these differences, each blood type has different characteristics that allow it to digest and absorb food in the most efficient manner for that particular gathering. To be healthy, we should all follow a diet that is appropriate for our blood type. Agglutination (thickening) happens when we consume foods that aren't good for our blood, and it continues in our bodies after that. Antibodies protect our bodies against outside intruders.

Our secure framework provides a variety of antibodies to protect us from outside substances. Every neutralizer is designed to bind to an antigen or substance that is foreign to it. When the body detects a trespasser, additional antibodies are produced to attack the intruder. A "gluing action" (agglutination) occurs when the antibody binds to the invader. As a result, the body has a better chance of removing these strange intruders. If, however, Similarly, when we consume foods that our bodies are unable to metabolize, we fight to make use of them, resulting in acid reflux, bulging, and vaporous distention.

The risk of illness is greatly reduced when you follow a proper eating routine that includes food for sustenance as well as specific upgrades tailored to your requirements. Appropriate dietary habits based on blood type, along with regular exercise, enable your immune system to function at its best. A strong, unbreakable structure might be the difference between a longer or shorter life span. Each blood classification has been seen to have a twenty-year future provided they follow the appropriate food regimen.

Type O, which accounts for nearly half of the population, was the most experienced and distinctive blood group. Men used to be meat hunters, and they now thrive on physical activity and a high-protein diet supplemented with leafy greens. Type Os have the thinnest blood, the safest framework (save for specific illnesses), the safest stomach corrosive, and the longest lifespan of all the blood types. The Os can separate high protein meals because to their solid stomach corrosive, and they can modify to eat almost anything. This corresponding solid stomach corrosive, on the other hand, has a detrimental side effect. When there is no food available or when food is not consumed at regular intervals, it might cause ulcers. Type Os should brush all day long since they are prone to stomach ulcers.

For a variety of reasons, the O has a higher life expectancy than some of the other blood types. Because of their thin blood, most Os are less susceptible to cardiovascular disease caused by blood clusters or the growth of very active Os who like high-intensity activities such as jogging and Tae-Bo. I was unable to participate in these activities due to my discomfort, so I joined a recreation center and decided to try out all of the programs available, including low impact, turning, salsa, Yoga, and Pilates. Overall, my aggravation was reduced by 90% after only two Yoga courses. I used to think Yoga was just for girls, but I was wrong. I have a lot of experience with Yoga and Pilates, and I am always facing new challenges. I set a goal for myself by taking a stand on my head, something I'd never done before. I just completed that challenge and now need handstands. We Os aren't easily won over.

Joint discomfort is another affliction that Type O suffers from. This infection attacks the edges of the joints, as well as the muscles, tendons, ligaments, and veins that surround them. Unfortunately, I, too, suffer from this ailment, but Yoga has shown to be really beneficial. With the various Yoga poses, you stir and stimulate all of the nerves and organs; some are designed to increase the flow of synovial liquid into the joints; the very liquid coming up short on this produces ligament discomfort.

The cause of this illness is unknown to medical research, however it is possible that the problem is due to an improper diet. White and red potatoes, squeezed orange, and dairy products in general seem to be the food types that trigger this illness.

Because of the variety of fast food options and advertising on starch eats less, people in today's society are more likely to gain weight effectively. Gluten, contained in raw grain and whole wheat products, is the major cause of weight gain for Os. Gluten lectins are proteins that bind to gluten and prevent it from being absorbed into the body.

Insulin digestion is slowed, preventing efficient energy usage. In contrast to other blood kinds, it obstructs the framework rather than invigorating it.

Weissberg, Steven M.D., and Joseph Christiano (1999). Your Bloodtype Holds the Key. Lake Mary, Florida is located in the state of Florida. Individual Nutrition USA, Inc. is a company that specializes in providing nutritional supplements to individuals

Section A Special Helps

The accuracy with which the fixings are estimated, the temperature at which the food is prepared, and the amount of time it takes to cook the food all contribute to successful cooking or baking. I recommend that you use the following to ensure that the heat and timing are correct:

To check the accuracy of your stove's heat, use a broiler thermometer.

A small clock with an alarm for any time interval up to an hour.

Using the right equipment is crucial for accurately measuring volume. Use graduated estimating spoons with sizes ranging from one-fourth teaspoon to one tablespoon to estimate dry fixings. A set with a one-eighth teaspoon is fantastic.

One-quarter, 33 percent, one-half, three-quarters, and one-cup graduated estimating cups

For estimating fluids, you'll need at least one two-cup standard glass-estimating cup. To avoid spilling the liquid, these cups should have the one-cup line beneath the top.

How to correctly measure:

Keep the glass estimating cup at eye level so you can double-check the total.

In one of the graduated measuring cups, measure the dry fixings.

Fill the cup almost to the brim, then smooth out the dry ingredients with the straight edge of a blade or spatula.

However, brown or date sugars, as well as fats, should be pressed in the cup rather than tapping the cup or packing flours in the estimating cup.

In the same way, measure the spoons. Using a straight edge, level out a spoonful of the item. Pour liquids and syrups into the spoon, but don't try to even them out.

In quarter-pounds, butter is stuffed. The wrapping paper is usually marked with estimates, but pay attention to how the paper is placed on the square. That's correct.

You should compensate for the inaccuracy by not wearing it unambiguously.

between the cookie sheet's edges and the inside walls of the oven

The majority of cookies should be baked for 5 to 15 minutes at 350°F to 425°F. Bake for 8 to 15 minutes at 325°F to 350°F for fruit, chocolate, and soft spice cookies.

Overcooking results in dry, hard cookies, so keep an eye on the baking time. Because of the thickness and size of the cookies, it's difficult to know exactly how long they'll take to bake. To see if the cookies are done, check them a few minutes before the suggested time.

Crisp cookies are ready when they have turned a light brown color. If the impression left by lightly touching the cookie's center does not disappear, the cookie is done.

Before removing the cookies from the baking sheet, allow them to cool slightly. They will continue to cook if you leave them on the pan for an extended period of time. Professionals recommend cooling the cookies on a wire rack, but I prefer to use paper towels.

After they've completely cooled, store in tightly covered containers. They will become soggy if you store them before they have fully cooled. Do not mix and match cookie types in the same container.

Cookies can be frozen for up to a year.

Oven Hours Meats Weight Temp Rib 4 - 10 lbs. 350°F 2 14 - 3 12 - 2 14 - 3 12 - 2 14 - 3 12 - 2 14 150\sTenderloin The weight ranges from 2 to 5 pounds. 425 Approximately 45-70 minutes 150

12 – 2 Tri-Tip 425 Approximately 40-45 minutes Round Tip 150 lbs. 350 calories per pound, 3 to 8 lbs. 2 14–3 12 hr 150

Round's eye 350 calories per pound, 2 to 3 lbs. 12:12 - 1:34 a.m. 150 BROILING:

The broiler should be preheated. To avoid flare-ups while cooking, trim the excess fat if desired. To keep the fat from curling, slash it along the edge of the meat. The top of the meat, in general, should be 2 to 4 inches away from the heat source. Broil on one side according to the chart below, season, and then flip and cook until done on the other side. Cut a small gash in the thickest part of the meat or near the bone to check for doneness, and note the color; "pink is typically medium."

Per side, inch steak

5 minutes rare, 6 minutes medium, 7 minutes rare, 7 minutes medium, 7 minutes rare

7-8 minutes, well-done

Per side, inch steak

Rare (16 minutes) Medium (18 minutes) Rare (16 minutes) Rare (16 minutes) Rare (16 minutes

20 minutes, well-done

PAN-BROILED STEAK: Pan broiling is recommended for steaks that are less than 1 inch thick. Heat the frying pan and coat it with a little of the rendered meat fat or olive oil. Season the meat, then turn and brown on the other side until juices appear in the unseared side. Pour any remaining juices out of the pan. When the steak has been browned, it is usually done. If not, reduce the heat and cook until the meat is done to your liking, turning once in a while.

Rib-Eye 34 inch Beef Cut Thickness T-Bone Porterhouse 34" Top Round Steak 34 inch Top Sirloin - Boneless Top Sirloin - Boneless Top Sirloin - Boneless Top Sirloin - Boneless Top Round Steak 34

T-Bone 1 inch Top Sirloin - Boneless Rib-Eye 1 inch Rib-Eye 1 inch Rib-Eye 1 inch Rib-Eye 1 inch Rib-Eye 1 inch Rib- 1 inch thick top round steak 1 inch thick bottom round steak 1 inch thick bottom round steak 1 inch thick bottom round

8–10 minutes to cook

11 – 13 minutes – 13 minutes – 12 minutes – 13 minutes – 12 minutes – 13 minutes – 12 minutes – 13 minutes

15 - 16 minutes, 17 - 20 minutes, 15 - 16 minutes, 17 - 20 minutes, 15 - 16 minutes, 17 - 20 minutes, 15 - 16 minutes COOKING WITH A MOIST HEAT

Grilled or pan-fried are two methods of cooking.

SIRLOIN: Tender cuts of beef that marinate beautifully.

Large boneless or boned sirloin steaks are available. They are available with a variety of bones and levels of tenderness. Pin bone steaks are the most tender, followed by flat, round, and wedge bone steaks in order of decreasing tenderness.

Sirloin Tip Roast is tender enough to roast on its own, but it tastes best when marinated.

Chapter 3

BENEFICIAL* GROCERIES FOR TYPE O MEALS

Let's go over some important points about buying and storing fish before we get into the cooking methods for fish.

Check the sell-by or use-by date on the label.

Check for ice crystals or freezer burns on frozen fillets or steaks before purchasing.

If you buy your fish fresh from the market, look for bright, bulging eyes, reddish gills, and elastic, firm flesh. Fish will always have an odor, but it should be fresh, clean, and pleasant, particularly around the gills and belly. If you've done all of the above and are still unsure if the fish is fresh, place it in a sink full of water. Fish will float if they're fresh.

You can be pretty sure you'll have enough fish for your meal if you stick to this rule of thumb.

4 people can be served from a pound of fish steaks 5 to 6 people can be served from a pound of fish fillets

About 3 and a half pounds of frozen fish will serve 3 to 5 people. When you buy fish, make sure you get home right away. After taking it out of the freezer compartment at the market, it should be refrigerated within 30 minutes. Cook or freeze the fish within 36 hours.

Fish that has been frozen can be stored for up to six months.

Defrost the fish for one day in the fridge or under cold running water. DON'T THAW THE FISH AT ROOM TEMPERATURE ON THE COUNTER.

Fish can be cooked frozen in the same way as a thick cut of meat, but the cooking time will be doubled.

If you buy fish brand new, make sure it's kept in a tight-fitting cooler bag. This will prevent the scent from lingering in your fridge.

When cleaning the fish before cooking, always use hot lathery water.

After each use and before using them for any other food preparation, wash the utensils and cutting sheets. This is to keep dangerous bacteria from spreading.

In the refrigerator, defrost and marinate. In light of the dangers of bacteria, it's worth repeating.

If you marinate fish for longer than 30 minutes in a citrus-based marinade, the fish will begin to cook in the marinade.

If you want to include the marinade in the sauce, make sure to boil it first.

Do not serve the meat on the same platter that it was served on before it was cooked.

It's simple to prepare fish. Baking, searing, and barbecuing/broiling are the three most commonly used methods.

A GREAT FISH TO GRILL OR BROIL Cod, halibut, perch, pike, rainbow trout, red snapper, shad, sole, sea bass, sturgeon, and swordfish are all excellent options.

Spices and herbs that enhance the flavor of various fish species include: Cumin Seeds with Basil Bay Leaves Rosemary Tarragon (curry powder)

Marjoram Thyme (Cayenne Pepper)

powdered chili Oregano *parsley

Before broiling, spray the searing rack or grill with nonstick cooking spray.

When grilling, keep the skin on the fish.

It's much easier to turn the fish without it falling apart or sticking to the grill if you have a barbecuing crate.

For added moisture, brush the fish with a marinade made with oil or lemon juice.

To keep the surface moist, baste the fish frequently while searing or barbecuing.

Cook the fish for 10 minutes for each inch of thickness measured from the thickest piece of meat.

If the fish is thicker than one inch, add or subtract time from the brief guideline: under 1 inch thick, cook in 12 minutes; north of 1 inch thick, add 5 minutes and cook for 15 minutes.

If you're using frozen fish, multiply the time by two, or 16-20 minutes per inch of thickness, starting with the thickest piece of meat. 9. Place 1 inch thick or less fish 2 to 4 crawls away from the heat source; thicker fish should be placed 5 to 6 crawls away from the broiler.

If the fish isn't exactly half an inch thick, don't turn it halfway through the cooking time.

Overcooking the fish will cause it to lose its flavor and become dry and extreme.

When the internal temperature of the fish reaches 145°F on a meat thermometer, or when a fork pierces the thickest piece of meat, the fish chips; the middle tissue should be hazy (a strong color).

If you're serving the fish in the same dish it was cooked in, make sure it's served quickly.

Before serving, let the fish rest for 3 to 4 minutes.

The surface of fish is delicate, and its flavor is delicate. As backups, serve fish with firm, bright crude vegetables, new green mixed greens, barbecued tomatoes or spinach, and velvety sauces. The vegetables and sauces will enhance the fish's flavor and presence.

Remember to garnish with parsley and a slice of lemon on each plate.

Try a little vinegar in the dishwater after you've made a fantastic meal and want to get rid of the strong smell. It will aid in the removal of unpleasant odors.

All of your ingredients should be organic, unprocessed, and uncooked. It's becoming easier to find these sound files on a regular basis. Most supermarkets now deliver eggs from cage-free hens and have a section in the produce department with a few organic items. Our neighborhood supermarket has a special "health foods" section that includes soy and rice milks, organic canned goods, cereals, pastas, and other items. Stock up on natural nuts, dried organic products, frozen vegetables and organic products, and store them in your cooler until you're ready to use them, until your neighborhood store has everything you need.

The following is a list of Os Beneficial Foods*, or foods that work like medicine. Keep these items in abundance in your storage space and use them often. Try to remember at least one of these food varieties for your dinner menu whenever you're planning your meals. Every recipe in this book contains at least one beneficial* ingredient, and they're all relatively easy to make. Nuts and seeds are two types of nuts and seeds that can be found in nature.

Os can get a good supply of vegetable protein from nuts and seeds. Because nuts are high in fat, they should be consumed in moderation if you're trying to lose weight.

Walnuts, Flaxseed, and Pepitas (Pumpkin Seeds).

Beans and legumes are a type of legume that can be eaten raw or cooked.

Beans and legumes play a minor role in the O diet.

Black-eyed Peas, Adzuki Bean

Grains, breads, and pastas are some of the most popular foods in the world.

Os don't do well with grains, bread, and pasta. Whole wheat items are not tolerated by operating systems because they contain lectins, which react with their blood and gastrointestinal systems, slowing legitimate ingestion of various food sources. Wheat, for the most part, puts the burden on Os, as the glutens in the raw grain slow O's metabolic cycles, causing the body to store the food as fat. The Essene and Ezekiel breads are hand-processed seed breads.

The gluten lectins that cause the problem in Os can be removed by the growing system, so these breads can be consumed. Furthermore, these breads are living foods, containing a variety of beneficial compounds.

In place of wheat flour, a variety of flours can be used. In the vast majority of the recipes in this section, spelt flour has been used to great effect. Some recipes can be substituted with oat flour, soy flour, or rice flour.

Essence is a term used to describe something that (Manna)

Vegetables

O's diet is incomplete without vegetables. The majority of vegetables are safe to eat, but be sure to read "The Avoids" list. Corn and potatoes, for example, are among the vegetables to avoid.

Artichokes, Broccoli, Chicory, Collard Greens, Dandelion, Escarole, Horseradish, Kale, Kelp, Kohlrabi, Okra, Onion,

Parsley, Pumpkin, Red/Cayenne Pepper, Romaine Lettuce, Spinach, Sweet Potatoes, Swiss Chard, Turnips

Fruits

Fruits are high in fiber, vitamins, and minerals. However, some fruits, such as oranges and tangerines, should be avoided, just as vegetables should. These have a high corrosive content, which causes digestive poisoning. Banana, Blueberry, Cherry, Fig, Guava, Mango, Pineapple, Plum, Prune, Plum, Prune

Juices and liquids are two types of liquids that can be consumed.

Juices contain the nutritional benefits of the fruits and vegetables from which they are squeezed, so choose from the list. Squeezes with a lot of basic substance, such as vegetable juice or dark cherry juice, are good choices. If you're trying to lose weight, pineapple juice is a great option because it's known to aid in water retention and bloating.

Pineapple, Prunus, and Black Cherry

Spices

Flavors, when chosen correctly, can have a significant impact on stomach-related and safe structures. Kelp, for example, is one of the most luxurious regular food sources, with around 30 minor components and significant minerals. It will aid the Os in directing their thyroid organ, which has a normally ineffective capacity, because it is a rich source of iodine. Hyperacidity, which can lead to ulcers, is also a common symptom of Type Os. The bladderwrack kelp's high fucose content protects the gastrointestinal lining, which helps to prevent ulcers.

Curry, Dulse, Ginger, Horseradish, Kelp (Bladderwrack), Parsley, Pepper/Cayenne, Turmeric

Chapter 1. Beverages

Os LACK OF BEVERAGE CHOICES

When I read with regards to our decisions in refreshments, I thought I 'd always be unable to drink as indicated by my blood classification O. Polishing off 2-3 jars of Diet Coke, 2-3 glasses of milk, and a nightcap glass of Pinot Gregio, or a jar of Coors Light, day by day put me in the classification of gradually ending it all; all that I drank behaved like a toxic substance as per D'Adamo's theory.

However, since I began this diet three months prior, I drink something like a liter of seltzer or shimmering water every day and have not had, or needed, a Diet Cola or a glass of milk. I feel that what my body required was the carbonation in the cola. I couldn't have ever accepted I could live without my cola; I bet you can too.

Since I had been drinking milk for a long time, I thought the weaning off of milk would likewise be amazingly troublesome.

I was exceptionally astounded to completely partake in the new sensations milk substitutes advertised. Rice milk is exceptionally sweet and the plain or chocolate is scrumptious. I regularly combine them as one for assortment and appreciate them either chilled or warmed. My sense of taste inclines toward the rice milk to soy milk, yet I use soy in cooking and on cereal. The rice milk is excessively sweet and has demolished a portion of the plans I attempted to substitute it in. Soy has worked entirely without fail. And afterward there is Blue Diamond Chocolate Almond milk; it's the best!

Merlot, a red wine which is viewed as "unbiased", has been a great substitute for the Pinot Gregio. Operating system will miss drinking the white wine with their fish, yet it's best not to drink any fluids while you eat in any case, as the fluids obstruct the stomach related process.

TRY TO DRINK AT LEAST HALF YOUR BODY WEIGHT IN OUNCES OF WATER DAILY OR A COMBINATION OF FRESH FRUIT JUICE AND WATER DAILY.

Chapter 4

ABOUT O's GRAINS, BREADS AND PASTAS

Being a bread nut, I was crushed when I discovered that Os were to keep away from wheat flour. I had been eating all the yummy entire wheat specialty breads for quite a long time. I even added the grand nutritious raw grain to food varieties for my family any place I could. I'd place some raw grain into a meat portion, on oats, in treats, cakes and biscuits. Any place flour was required in a formula, I'd substitute raw grain for a piece of the entire wheat flour.

However, in the beyond couple of years, I have seen that my framework tries to avoid the wheat items however much I do, presumably originating from the issues that Os have with wheat.

Wheat contains a lectin that responds to the O's blood and gastrointestinal system, disrupting the appropriate ingestion of gainful food varieties. The glutens in the wheat impede the metabolic cycles causing wasteful or slow digestion. This makes the food all the more leisurely proselyte to energy, and you got it, stores it as fat.

While searching for an option in contrast to my beloved breads and flour I could use to prepare with, I was acquainted with a few new food varieties that are awesome. The Ezekiel 4:9 bread and spelt flour will presumably turn into your staple food sources, while buckwheat, soy, oat and rice flours will be your choices for baking flour, pasta and cereals. Assuming that you are utilized to entire wheat breads, you will observe Ezekiel bread totally flavorful, particularly the raisin bread. In these grew seed breads, the growing system annihilates the gluten lectins that bring O's hardship. They are live food sources with numerous useful proteins intact.

Ezekiel bread has been utilized with incredible achievement in every one of the plans in this book that require bread. What's more fortunately Ezekiel bread is easy to find. protein than wheat (from 10 to 25 percent more prominent than the normal assortments of business wheat), higher in B complex nutrients, basic and complex sugars. Spelt has high water dissolvability, so the body effectively ingests the supplements. It contains unique carbs (mucopolysaccharides), which are a significant element in blood coagulating (which Os need assistance in) and animating the body's invulnerable framework. Spelt items are extraordinary for competitors who need to carb load for rivalry, on account of the great degree of complex carbs.

Os should restrict their utilization of grains, breads and pasta to 6 servings each week, however your decisions can be"delicious" and sound, so appreciate them when you can.

BANANA APRICOT BREAD

1/3 cup margarine 2/3 cup honey

3 eggs

cup pounded bananas * ¼ cup harsh soy milk (1 teaspoon lemon juice and enough milk to make 1 cup, let stand somewhere around 15 minutes).

cups spelt flour 1 cup apricots

½ cup slashed pecans * 2 teaspoons baking powder 1 teaspoon baking soda

½ teaspoon cinnamon

tablespoons spelt flour 2 tablespoons butter

1/3 cup brown sugar ½ teaspoon cinnamon

½ cup finely hacked pecans *

1 egg ¼ cup relaxed butter

½ cup soy milk

1 cup washed and depleted blueberries

1 tablespoon finely hacked pecans * ¼ teaspoon cinnamon

½ tablespoon brown sugar

Steps: Combine the flour, baking powder, salt and sugar.

Cream the egg and spread, and afterward add the milk and beat until smooth. Don't over beat.

Make a well in the focal point of the flour combination and add the creamed blend at the same time to the flour. Mix until recently soaked. Player ought to be lumpy.

Carefully overlay the depleted blueberries into the batter.

Spoon into paper cup lined biscuit tins. Makes around 10 muffins.

Mix the garnish fixings and sprinkle on the highest point of the muffins.

Bake at 375 degrees for 20 to 25 minutes. BANANA DATE BREAD

3 pounded bananas * ¼ cup canola oil

½ cup sugar 2 eggs

1½ cup spelt flour ¾ teaspoon baking powder

½ teaspoon baking soda

½ teaspoon ocean salt

½ cup ground flax seeds * ¼ cup entire flax seed *

½ cup slashed pitted dates Steps:

Beat together the bananas, oil, sugar, and eggs.

Combine the flour, baking powder, baking pop, salt, ground flax, and entire flax.

Gradually add the flour combination into the banana blend, and afterward overlap in the dates.

Pour the hitter into an 8x4 inch portion pan.

Bake at 350 degrees for 55-an hour, or until a toothpick stuck into the focal point of the portion comes out clean.

CHERRY NUT BREAD

1 cup brown sugar ¼ cup butter

egg cups spelt flour

2½ teaspoons baking powder 1 teaspoon salt

1 little container maraschino cherries *, depleted (hold the juice), and cut up ½ cup pecans * 1 cup of the saved cherry juice, in addition to enough soy milk to approach

one cup Steps: Cream the sugar and butter.

Add the egg, flour, baking powder, and salt to the creamed blend, and afterward crease in the cherries and nuts.

Add the cherry milk then again with the flour to the creamed combination, mix just until clammy. Don't over blend. Fill a portion pan.

Bake at 350 degrees for an hour, or until a toothpick tells the truth when jabbed in the center. PRUNE BREAD

1½ cups spelt flour

½ teaspoon baking soda

½ teaspoon ocean salt

½ cup sugar

egg marginally beaten tablespoons liquefied butter

½ cup soy milk

½ cup hacked cooked prunes * ½ cup prune juice *

tablespoons cleaved pecans * 1 tablespoon sugar

Steps: Combine the flour, baking pop, salt, and sugar.

Mix the egg, spread, milk, prunes, and juice.

Combine flour and the fluid together and blend at medium speed for around 2 minutes.

Pour the hitter into a 9x5 inch portion pan.

Mix the pecans and sugar and sprinkle over the batter.

Bake at 375 degrees for around 40-50 minutes, or until the toothpick jabbed in the middle comes out clean.

PUMPKIN CRANBERRY BREAD

cups spelt flour 1½ cups sugar

1½ cups brown sugar teaspoons baking powder 2 teaspoons baking soft drink 1½ teaspoons cinnamon ¼ teaspoon clove 2 teaspoons salt 4 somewhat beaten eggs 1 cup canola oil 2/3 cup water

15oz. can pumpkin *

cups entire cranberries

tablespoons hacked pecans * 1 tablespoon sugar

6 tablespoons dissolved spread 1 teaspoon vanilla 2 cups spelt flour 2 teaspoons baking soda

1 teaspoon lemon juice + soy milk to approach ¼ cup let set 5+ minutes. 2/3 cup carob chips

½ cup hacked pecans * 1 tablespoon finely slashed pecans * ½ tablespoon brown sugar

Steps: Cream the bananas, sugar, and eggs until well mixed.

Stir in the margarine and vanilla.

Add the flour, baking pop and acrid milk to the creamed combination, mix just until recently mixed. Don't over mix.

Stir in the carob and walnuts.

Mix the fixing pecans and brown sugar.

Put paper cups into a biscuit tin and spoon the player into the biscuit cups until 2/3 full. Makes around 15 muffins.

Sprinkle every biscuit with the a portion of the toppings.

Bake at 350 degrees for 20 minutes, or until a tooth pick jabbed in the middle comes out clean.

Let biscuits sit for around 5 minutes, then, at that point, eliminate from the pan. BLUEBERRY MUFFINS

1¾ cups spelt flour

2½ teaspoons baking powder

¼ teaspoon ocean salt ½ cup sugar

1 egg ¼ cup relaxed butter

½ cup soy milk

1 cup washed and depleted blueberries

1 tablespoon finely cleaved pecans * ¼ teaspoon cinnamon

½ tablespoon brown sugar

Steps: Combine the flour, baking powder, salt and sugar.

Cream the egg and spread, and afterward add the milk and beat until smooth.

Don't over beat.

Make a well in the focal point of the flour blend and add the creamed combination at the same time to the flour. Mix until recently saturated. Hitter ought to be lumpy.

Carefully crease the depleted blueberries into the batter.

Spoon into paper cup lined biscuit tins. Makes around 10 muffins.

Mix the garnish fixings and sprinkle on the highest point of the muffins.

Bake at 375 degrees for 20 to 25 minutes. SPINACH OMELET

1 tablespoon olive oil * ½ cup slashed onion * 1 cup hacked red pepper *

1 cup cleaved portabella mushroom 6 cups crude spinach * 1 minced clove garlic 1 teaspoon oregano

½ teaspoon iodized ocean salt ¼ teaspoon cayenne pepper * 1 tablespoon butter

6 beaten eggs

¼ cup feta cheese

¼ cup destroyed mozzarella 2

tablespoons parsley * 1 tablespoon cut Greek or Spanish olives.

Steps: Heat the oil in a skillet and sauté the onion and pepper until the onion is translucent.

Add the mushrooms, spinach, garlic and oregano until the spinach shrivels, or for around 5 minutes. Channel the liquid.

Season with salt and pepper.

In a different skillet, dissolve the spread and afterward mix in the eggs. Cook the eggs until they are dry and cushy, and afterward flip and cook for a couple of moments more until the base is golden.

Once the eggs are great, cut the omelet down the middle. Add the vegetables and feta on the highest point of one portion of the omelet, and afterward cover with the other half. Sprinkle the top with mozzarella and cover the skillet. Proceeding to cook until the cheddar is melted. 6. Sprinkle with parsley and top with olives.

Chapter 3. Appetizers and Snacks

DIP OF ARTICHOKE

1 cup soy Parmesan cheese (ground) 1 cup mayonnaise made from canola

14 oz. depleted and hacked artichoke hearts * 1 14 oz. green chilies depleted and slashed

cloves of garlic, minced

2 tblsp. green onions, diced 2 tblsp. chopped tomatoes

Steps: Toss all of the ingredients together, except the onions and tomatoes, and spoon into a 9-inch pie plate.

Bake for 20 to 25 minutes at 350 degrees, or until lightly browned. 3. Garnish with onions and tomatoes before serving.

ONION IN FULL FLORENCE

4 extremely large, stripped onions (approximately 4 inch width) * 412 cup spelt flour 2 teaspoons paprika teaspoons garlic salt 1 tsp. sea salt 1/4 tsp. cayenne pepper * 112 tablespoons softened margarine * 2 cups pumpkin seeds 12 tbsp. salt

Chapter 4. Salads, Soups and Stews Salads

BENEFICIAL SALAD

1 stripped and cut banana *\s¼ cup pineapple juice *

medium size stripped and cut guava * 1 cup pineapple chunks\stablespoons sugar 1/8 teaspoon ginger *\s½ cup canola mayonnaise (from adequate ingredients) (from adequate ingredients) ¼ cup pineapple juice * Cinnamon

Steps:\sSprinkle the bananas with pineapple juice.

Combine the organic products in a serving bowl.

Mix the ginger and sugar, and afterward sprinkle over the fruit.

Mix the mayo and juice. Mix until smooth.

Sprinkle with cinnamon. BLACK EYED PEA SALAD

6 enormous cloves squashed garlic

½ cup cleaved red onion *\s2 tablespoons finely hacked parsley * 2 tablespoons finely slashed dill

½ cup hacked red chime pepper * 1 teaspoon ocean salt\s¼ teaspoon cayenne pepper *\s¼ cup lemon juice

1 tablespoon olive oil *

¼ cup feta cheese 1 tomato quartered

1 tablespoon pine nuts\shardboiled egg quartered

Toss all the ingredients together. Serve with your favorite dressing. GARDENBURGER SALAD

¼ teaspoon olive oil *\sone inch thick slices of onion *

2 Gardenburgers, any style of acceptable ingredients

¼ cup shredded mozzarella cheese 1

large portabella mushroom 1/8 tablespoon olive oil * 1 tablespoon butter

4 romaine lettuce leaves torn in bite size pieces * 4 escarole leaves torn in bite size pieces *\s½ cup chopped red pepper *\s¼ cup pine nuts

½ cup chopped tomato

Steps:\sTear the romaine and spinach leaves into bite size pieces.

Toss all the ingredients together with your favorite dressing. HI PRO SALAD 8 spinach leaves torn in bite size pieces * 2\sromaine leaves torn in bite size pieces * 4 escarole leaves torn in bite size pieces * 1 tablespoon pumpkin seeds *\s10 chopped walnuts * 1/3 cup feta cheese

½ cup shredded mozzarella cheese 1 egg sliced\s½ teaspoon kelp *

Toss all of the ingredients together with your favorite dressing. PARSLEY SALAD 2 tablespoons olive oil *\s1 cup chopped portabella mushrooms

bunch green onions *\s½ cup chives\sbunches chopped parsley * 1 tablespoon lemon juice *\s½ teaspoon sea salt

Steps:\sSauté mushrooms in oil.

Add and heat the green onions and chives.

Add the parsley to the onions and heat.

Add the lemon juice and salt to taste.

Serve warm or cold. SPINACH SALAD

2 tablespoons flaxseeds *\stablespoons sesame seeds 1 teaspoon sugar\stablespoons chicken broth 2 teaspoons Tamari\s½ teaspoon kelp *

2 tablespoons olive oil *\s1 lb. washed fresh leaves of spinach *

1 cup walnuts *

1 cup chopped dates 1 cup raisins

1 cup chopped celery

2-3 tablespoons canola mayonnaise (from acceptable ingredients) (from acceptable ingredients) ¼ teaspoon cinnamon Romaine lettuce *

Steps:\sSprinkle the bananas with lemon juice.

Add the fruits, nuts, and celery together.

Mix the mayonnaise with the cinnamon and then add to the salad.

Serve about ½ cupful of salad on a leaf of romaine lettuce. WALDORF SALAD 4 romaine lettuce leaves * 2\scups chopped apples

½ cup chopped celery

½ cup sliced banana *\s¼ cup raisins

¼ cup walnuts *

1½ tablespoons canola mayonnaise, from acceptable ingredients 1/8 teaspoon cinnamon Steps:\sMix fruits and nuts.

Mix the mayonnaise and cinnamon.

Toss the mayo with the fruits and nuts.

Serve about ½ cupful of salad on a leaf of romaine* lettuce.

Soups

1 cup soy yogurt or soy sour cream Steps:

Bring water and bouillon cube to boil in deep pot.

Add the remaining ingredients, except the yogurt, and boil for 15 minutes until frothy. Remove froth and disard.

Reduce the heat and simmer for 2 hours, or until smooth.

Pour in a blender and process until the desired consistency.

Serve with a spoonful of yogurt. CREAMY BEAN SOUP

1 cup dried adzuki beans * soaked overnight and drained. 3½ cups water

2½ teaspoons salt

1 cup diced butternut squash

½ teaspoon grated ginger root *\s½ teaspoon cinnamon

1 tablespoon chopped fresh parsley * Steps:

Put the beans in salted water and bring to a boil, and then reduce the heat and simmer, covered, for 1 hour.

Stir in the squash, ginger, and simmer 30 minutes longer.

Pour into a blender and process until the desired consistency. 3. Garnish with parsley. CREAMY ESCAROLE SOUP

¼ lb. white beans 5 cups water

6 beef bouillon cubes *\s

3 tablespoons olive oil *\s2 tablespoons minced garlic * 1 chopped onion *

2 cups chopped escarole\sSea salt and cayenne pepper * to taste\s¼ mozzarella cheese

Steps:\sSoak the beans in water overnight. Drain.

Combine beans, water, and bullion in a pot, cover and cook over medium for 30 minutes, or until the beans are soft.

Heat the olive oil in a large pot and sauté the garlic and onion until the onion is soft, about 5 minutes, stirring occasionally.

Add the escarole and simmer until it is wilted, about another 10 minutes.

Add the beans, broth, salt, and pepper to the escarole. Cover and simmer 20 minutes more.

Put in a blender and process until the desired consistency.

Garnish with cheese.

CREAMY SWISS CHARD SOUP

2 tablespoons butter\slb. washed Swiss chard *

tablespoons spelt flour 1 can beef broth *\s½ cup soy milk

Sea salt and cayenne pepper * to taste\s¼ cup shredded mozzarella cheese

Steps:\sMelt the butter in a skillet.

Separate the chard leaves from the stems. Chop the leaves and the stems separately.

Add the stems to the melted butter, cover and cook for 3-4 minutes. Then stir in the leaves and cook 3-4 minutes more.

Next, sprinkle the leaves with the flour and stir until blended.

Gradually blend in the broth and milk. Cook and stir until slightly thickened.

Pour the soup in a blender and process until the desired consistency.

Season to taste with salt and pepper, and garnish with mozzarella cheese. ONION SOUP

6 cups thinly sliced onions * 1/3 cup butter

cloves crushed garlic 1 teaspoon sugar

10½ oz. cans consume beef bouillon * 1 teaspoon sea salt

1/8 teaspoon cayenne pepper *\s

½ teaspoon paprika

¼ cup shredded mozzarella

Steps:\sCook the onion, okra, pepper, and celery in the butter in a skillet over low heat for 5 minutes.

Add the tomatoes, tapioca, sugar, paprika, and water.

Simmer for about 1 hour.

Add salt and pepper.

Cook rice according to the packaged directions.

Served over a heaping bowl of rice.

Chapter 5. Vegetables

HOW TO COOK BENEFICIAL* VEGETABLES

VEGETABLE

Artichoke HOW TO PREPARE

Wash, trim stems, and remove any discolored outer leaves.

Beet Greens (prepare as spinach) (prepare as spinach)

Thoroughly wash in cool water. Cut off any roots and remove damaged portions and large veins. Tear or cut up large leaves.

Broccoli Wash and remove

the outer leaves and tough parts of the stalks. Cut lengthwise into uniform spears.

Or, break off the HOW TO COOK

Cover the\sartichokes with boiling salted\swater. Boil until a leaf pulls out easily.

Use raw in salads.

water until tender.

ARTICHOKES

4 quarts boiling\swater 4 artichokes\s*\s4 tablespoons apple cider vinegar 4 tablespoons olive oil * 2 bay leaves

12 whole peppercorns

2 teaspoons salt

1 cup canola mayonnaise, from acceptable ingredients 2 teaspoons apple cider vinegar 1 teaspoon parsley *\s¼ teaspoon dill weed 1/8 teaspoon tarragon

Steps:\sClip the thorns off the tips of the artichoke leaves.

Boil the water, then add all the ingredients to the water, lower heat, cover and cook over medium heat for 45 to 50 minutes, or until the leaves pull off easily.

Mix all the mayonnaise ingredients together and let sit about an hour to blend the flavors.

Serve hot or cold.

Serve with mayonnaise dip.

HOW TO EAT AN ARTICHOKE

Dip the leaves in sauce one at a time.

The tender end is pulled through the teeth, and then discard the leaf.

Continue to eat unit the light colored core of young leaves appears, pull this up with one movement and discard.

Lift out the fuzzy center and discard.

Eat the yummy heart. BAKED SWEET POTATOES 2/3 cup honey

½ cup butter\steaspoon sea salt 8 sliced sweet\spotatoes * Steps:

Combine the honey, butter, and salt.

Layer the potato slices and honey in a greased baking dish.

Bake at 350 degrees for 30 minutes. Baste frequently. BEET GREENS

½ tablespoon canola mayonnaise 1 teaspoon dried\s

mustard\scups beet greens washed with the large veins and damaged portions removed * 2 tablespoons butter

1 teaspoon grated onion *\s¼ teaspoon sea salt\s1 tablespoon grated horseradish *

½ cup soy sour cream Steps:\sMix the mayonnaise and the mustard.

Heat butter in a skillet and add all the ingredients but the sour cream. Cover and steam 3-5 minutes, or until the leaves are wilted.

Removed from heat and add the sour cream. BEET SOUFFLE\sButter

3 tablespoons vegan parmesan cheese 2 cooked peeled and sliced beets\scup sautéed chopped beet greens *\s¼ cup chopped onion *

a couple of teaspoons of butter

2 tablespoons oat flour

¾ cup hot chicken broth

½ cup shredded mozzarella cheese 3 egg yolks

4 egg whites\s¼ teaspoon cayenne

pepper * Vegan parmesan cheese

Steps:\sButter a 1 quart soufflé dish. Sprinkle the bottom with 3 tablespoons parmesan cheese.

Place the beets evenly over butter on the bottom of the dish. 3. In a saucepan, melt the butter and stir in the flour.

Add the broth to the pan and continue to cook until slightly thickened. Transfer to a larger bowl.

Add the greens, onion, and the remaining cheese to the broth. 6. In a separate bowl, beat the egg yolks; blend them with the beet

greens.

Beat the egg whites until they form peaks. Fold into the bowl with the other ingredients; add\s

the pepper. Blend well.

Transfer all to the buttered soufflé dish. Sprinkle with additional parmesan cheese.

Preheat the oven to 350°F and bake the soufflé for 30 minutes, or until golden. TURNS IN WATER

6 medium potatoes, peeled and cubed

2 tblsp butter * turnips lemon juice, 1 tablespoon

2 TBS PARSLEY, CRUMBLED

12 tsp paprika + 12 tsp cayenne

1. Boil a small amount of salted water and cook the turnips in it. Boil for 20 to 30 minutes, or until the vegetables are tender, covered in the pan. Well-drained 2. Melt the butter, then stir in the lemon juice and parsley.

thoroughly.

3. Drizzle the turnips with the seasoned butter and season with pepper and paprika. CHEESE AND BROCCOLI * 1 inch boiling water * 1 large head of broccoli flowerets

2 tablespoons 12 teaspoon salt

12 cup soy milk 12 tablespoons butter

1 cup shredded mozzarella

12 tsp. sodium bicarbonate

paprika, 14 tsp

* 12 teaspoon dry mustard 1/8 teaspoon cayenne pepper

* Papri ka Parsle y Papri ka Parsle y Papri ka Parsle

Steps: In a covered pot, steam the broccoli spears or buds for 10 minutes in water.

Drain the broccoli and season with salt when it's finished. 3. In a saucepan, melt the butter, then whisk in the flour until smooth. 4. Gradually stir in the milk until the mixture is smooth. When the sauce is smooth, add the cheese and spices, stirring constantly until the cheese is melted.

Pour the cheese sauce over the broccoli in a serving dish. 7. Add more paprika and parsley if desired.

GRATINIZED BROCCOLI

* 1 inch boiling water + 1 large bunch of broccoli flowerets

12 teaspoon sea salt (iodized) 112 cup Ezekiel

breadcrumbs

melted butter (34) cup 1 12 teaspoon parsley * 1 12 teaspoon curry powder * 34 teaspoon paprika

12 tsp powdered garlic 12 c. mozzarella cheese, shredded
Steps:

In a covered pot with water, steam the broccoli spears or buds for 10 minutes.

Drain the broccoli, season it with salt, and place it in a casserole dish when it's finished.

After browning the breadcrumbs in butter, add the spices and mix well.

Bread crumbs should completely cover the broccoli. 5. Spread the cheese evenly over the breadcrumbs and broil until the cheese is melted and golden.

PARSLEY IN BUTTER

parsley, 4 lbs.

Ezekiel bread, diced 4 garlic cloves, crushed to taste, sea salt

butter (12 cup)

Step 1: Rinse and chop the parsley.

Put the parsley, butter, and garlic in a pan with a little water. Bring to a boil, then reduce to a low heat and cook until the vegetables are wilted, about 15 minutes; drain.

Toss in a pinch of sea salt and adjust the seasoning to taste.

Cover the cooked vegetables with the bread in a serving dish. SOY SAUCE FOR COLLARD GREENS

collard greens, 3 lbs.

soy sauce, 3 tblsp * 1 tablespoon sesame seeds 2 tablespoons olive oil garlic cloves, crushed 2

sugar 1 tbsp

1 tablespoon vinegar made from apple juice

* 2 tblsp. butter * 1 tblsp.

In a skillet, cook the chicory.

Sprinkle the chicory with the mixture of salt, pepper, honey, and lemon juice.

Spread butter on the chicory.

Just cover the chicory with a small amount of water. Heat the skillet, covered, until it reaches a boil. Uncover the skillet and cook, stirring occasionally, until the water has almost completely evaporated, leaving only syrup.

The chicory should then be browned in the syrup until it is well-coated. PARSNIPS and KALE are two of the most popular vegetables in the world. 1 pound onions, chopped

* 1 tablespoon olive oil * 1 cup parsnips, cut

rosemary (12 teaspoon)

* 14 teaspoon curry powder * 1/8 teaspoon cayenne pepper 1 cup crumbled cheddar mozzarella 4 colossal red peppers

Steps: Cook the rice according to the package directions, substituting sauce and water for the liquid.

Remove the tops and discard the seeds from the peppers.

When the meat is carmelized, channel off the fat by browning it with the onion, carrot, and garlic until the onion is clear. 4. Combine the rice, meat, spices, and cheese in a large mixing bowl.

The meat sauce should be stuffed into the peppers.

Cook for 30 to 35 minutes, or until the pepper is cooked, in a covered baking dish at 350 degrees.

COLLARD GREENS WITH SAUCE

2 tablespoons olive oil * 2 tablespoons hacked garlic cloves * 3 lbs. cleaved collard greens 12 tsp. salt from the sea

Remove the greens' stems and discard them. Before cooking, soak the greens in water to remove any sand.

In a skillet, heat the oil and cook the garlic for a few minutes.

Mix in the greens for 5 minutes, or until they are wilted. 4. Add salt and pepper to taste. DANDELION GREENS IN SAUCE

butter (four tablespoons)

4 tbsp. fresh parsley * 1 garlic clove, minced 1 tablespoon pimientos * lb. washed, hacked, and absorbed salted water dandelion greens * 1 teaspoon ocean salt 14 + teaspoon cayenne pepper

1. In a skillet, melt the margarine before adding the parsley, garlic, salt, and pepper. 3 minutes to fry Cook for 4 minutes after adding the pimientos.

3. Stir in the dandelion greens and cook for 5 minutes, or until they are tender.

tender.

KOHLRABI SAUTEED

kohlrabi that has been stripped of its leaves and managed

14 cup margarine 1 onion, chopped

1 tsp. marjoram (dried) 1 tsp basil powder

Grate the kohlrabi and then salt it. Allow 30 minutes for the kohlrabi to drain in a colander before crushing the water out.

In a skillet, melt the butter and cook the onions until they are translucent.

Stir in the kohlrabi and onions, reduce the heat to low, cover, and cook for 10 minutes. Cook for another 2 minutes after revealing and turning the heat up to medium.

Herbs can be added.

MUSHROOMS with SPINACH

34 cup hacked portabella mushrooms * 1 tablespoon olive oil * 1 cleaved red pepper * 1 slashed red onion * 1 garlic clove, minced 6 cups raw steamed spinach oregano, 1 tblsp.

beaten eggs, 6

1 pound of feta a quarter cup

Steps: In a skillet, cook the pepper, onion, and mushrooms until soft.

Cook for 3 minutes, or until the spinach has withered.

Add the eggs and mix well. Mix into the spinach and cook slowly, like an omelet, until it is 12 minutes done, dry, and brilliant on the bottom.

Sprinkle feta evenly over the spinach, overlap, and cook until crisp on the bottom.

Parsley can be added as a finishing touch. CHARD BAKE IN SWISS

Swiss chard, washed, 3 lbs.

Butter, 14 pound

* 2 garlic cloves, minced 1 diced onion

12 tsp. salt from the sea

paprika, 1 tblsp. nutmeg (1/8 tsp.)

* 12 pound destroyed mozzarella cheddar * 1/8 teaspoon cayenne Steps:

Remove the stems and trim the leaves from them. Make strips out of the leaves.

Heat the spread until it becomes effervescent in a large pot. Combine the onion and garlic in a medium-sized mixing bowl. 2–3 minutes in a hot pan.

Put the spinach in the pot. salt Cover and steam for 5 minutes, or until the vegetables are completely withered. Heat should be avoided.

Grease a goulash casserole dish that can be used in the oven.

Using a large spoon, spread a large amount of the cheddar cheese over the bottom half of the pizza.

casserole.

Swiss chard should be added at this point. Paprika, nutmeg, and pepper are sprinkled over the top.

The remaining mozzarella should be placed on top.

Bake for about 20 minutes at 350 degrees, or until the cheddar begins to bubble. CASSEROLE (TURNIP) 3 cups turnips, washed, peeled, and diced

1 teaspoon sea salt 1 cup water

butter tblsp

brown sugar (1 tablespoon)

12 tsp sodium

1/8 to 14% soy milk

* 1 cup Ezekiel delicate breadcrumbs * 14 cup slashed onions 2 quail

Boil turnips for about 20 minutes, or until tender, in a small amount of water.

Turnips should be drained completely.

Combine the turnips, spread, earthy colored sugar, salt, and enough soy milk to achieve a smooth consistency.

Then whip the pounded turnips with the breadcrumbs, onions, and eggs until smooth. In a goulash dish, combine all of the ingredients.

Bake for 35 minutes at 375°F.

Chapter 6. Meats

BEEF HEART and VEGETABLES

4 lbs. hamburger heart *

¼ cup spelt flour 1 teaspoon ocean salt

1 teaspoon garlic powder

½ teaspoon cayenne pepper *

3 tablespoons spread 1 cleaved onion

2 hacked carrots 1 slashed yam * 2 teaspoons thyme 1 cup meat broth ½ cup red wine

Steps: 1. Wash the heart and eliminate any fat and supply routes. Cut the heart fifty-fifty, and afterward cut it in ½ inch thick slices. 2. Dredge the heart in the flour, salt, and pepper.

3. Heat the margarine in a skillet over medium-high hotness and brown the heart cuts for around 30 to 45 seconds for every side. 4. Stir in the onion, carrots, potato, thyme, stock, and wine. Decrease hotness and stew for 1 hour longer.

BUFFALO STEAK

1½ cups olive oil * 3 minced garlic cloves ¾ cup dry red wine

½ teaspoon cayenne

pepper * 4 8oz. bison steaks * 1 teaspoon paprika *

cup canola or olive oil * Salt and cayenne pepper * to

taste Steps: Wash the sweetbread and dispose of any tacky tendons that hold it together. Cut in 1 inch pieces.

Combine the flour and flavors, and afterward dig the sweetbread pieces in the carefully prepared flour.

Heat the oil in a skillet and fry the sweetbreads until brilliant brown, turning once. Channel on paper towel.

Seasoning with salt and pepper.

1 cup slashed tomatoes

½ cup cleaved celery cup hacked red pepper *

tablespoons dissolved margarine 2 tablespoons spelt flour ¾ + or - cup soy milk 1 teaspoon ocean salt

1/8 teaspoon cayenne pepper * ¼ teaspoon

paprika Parsley *

Steps: Dredge the liver in flour.

2 In a skillet, brown the liver rapidly in 3 tablespoons butter.

Add the salt and vegetables, cover the dish and stew over low hotness for around 20 minutes.

Remove the liver and vegetables from the container. Cover to keep warm.

Melt 2 tablespoons spread in the container, and afterward add the flour. Mix until smooth.

Then add the milk and the flavors to the glue and mix until thickened.

Add the liver and vegetables to the sauce.

Sprinkle each presenting with parsley. SWEET and SOUR BEEF HEART

1 enormous meat heart, split and trim * Water to cover the heart

1 teaspoon ocean salt 1 cleaved onion * 1 straight leaf hacked stem of celery

butter tblsp

2 tablespoons spelt flour 1 tablespoon brown sugar tablespoon pineapple juice *

Steps: 1. Put the heart in a skillet and cover with water, and afterward add the salt, onion, cove leaf, and celery. Cook for 60 minutes; cool and eliminate the heart and vegetables. Dispose of the vegetables. 2. Trim the loss off the heart and solid shape the meat.

Brown the spread and the flour in the skillet, cook gradually until medium earthy colored tone; mixing constantly.

Add the sugar and squeeze to the flour and mix until smooth. 5. Return the heart to the container and stew 15 to 20 minutes more. TRI-TIP ROAST WITH PINEAPPLE MARINADE 5 lbs. tri-tip broil *

CHUNKY PINEAPPLE MARINADE tablespoons olive oil * 1 daintily cut onion *

¼ cup apple juice vinegar 2 cups hacked pineapple ¼ cup limeade

¼ cup slashed red pepper * ¼ cup honey

1/8 teaspoon cloves

cup basmati rice cups pineapple juice *

¼ cup cleaved nuts * 2 teaspoons olive

oil * ¾ cup hacked onions * 1 squashed clove garlic

½ cups raisins ¼ cup slashed apricots

Steps: Heat the oil and sauté the onion in it for around 5 minutes, or until translucent.

Add the leftover fixings and cook 5 minutes longer.

Pour the marinade over the meal and marinate for no less than 3 hours, or overnight.

Cook the rice as indicated by the headings on the bundle, involving the pineapple for the liquid.

Toast the pecans in a skillet. Shake the skillet regularly until the pecans are brilliant brown. Eliminate and set aside.

Sauté the oil, onion, and garlic to the skillet. Cook around 5 minutes, or until the onion starts to become brilliant brown. 7. Add cooked rice, raisins, and apricots to the onion blend. Mix over low hotness until combine.

8. Remove the dish from the marinade and barbecue for 30 to 40 minutes on a covered barbecue, or in the oven.

Do not overcook. It is best cooked at medium hotness and may look underdone when it is prepared to eat. Utilizing a meat thermometer gets it perfect.

Let it sit for around 5-10 minutes before carving.

Serve the tri tip with the rice. VENISON MEAT BALLS

4 cuts cubed Ezekiel bread

½ cup soy milk

1 egg slashed onion * teaspoons hacked cloves garlic 2 tablespoons oregano 3 tablespoons mint leaves 1 teaspoon ocean salt ¼ teaspoon cayenne pepper * 1 lb. ground venison * ¼ cup parsley *

Steps: Combine the bread morsels and milk; let stand 5 minutes.

Then add every one of the leftover fixings. For well.

Shape into 1 inch meat balls and set on a lubed baking pan.

Bake at 350 degrees for 10 minutes.

Chapter 6

GLOSSARY OF BASS TERMS

Surface is firm, fat content is reasonable, and the taste is sweet. Skin may be eaten. Broil, grill, sauté, poach, or steam your food.

Blackfish, Grouper, Red Snapper, Rockfish, Sea Bass, and Swordfish are all good substitutes.

BASS, SEA: Tender white tissue with a solid surface, low to moderate fat content, and a mild taste. The skin of an ocean bass may be eaten and is considered delectable.

Broil, grill, sear, reheat, or steam

Cod, Grouper, Haddock, Ocean Roost, Red Snapper, Striped Bass, Tilefish are also good substitutes. COD: Firm, flaky, and mildly flavored cod.

Bake, sear, deep-fry, grill, sear, poach, or sauté Treat on a regular basis. Haddock, Hake, Hoki, Pollock, Whiting are all good substitutes.

HALIBUT: White meat that is solid, well finished, lean, and close-grained. Braises, sears, grills, poaches, cooks, sautés, and steams

Cod, Dogfish, Flatfish, Haddock, Turbot are also good substitutes.

PERCH: Somewhat flaky, moderately stiff.

Bake, cook, deep-fry, grill, sear, poach, or sauté PIKE: Meat that is white and flaky.

Bake, sear, sauté, grill, or simmer are all options.

RAINBOW TROUT: Tender, flaky, delicate, mild, sensitive taste with a nutlike undertone. Prepare via sear, grilling, sautéing, or smoking.

Arctic Char, Salmon are good substitutes.

RED SNAPPER: Firm but not too so, with a modest fat content and a beautiful drop. Prepare by searing, frying, poaching, or sautéing. Treat yourself while you're cooking.

Titlefish may be used as a substitute.

SHAD: Extremely hard, heavy in fat, and delicately sweet. Use filets that have been deboned. Prepare by cooking, frying, or poaching. Blackfish, bluefish, mackerel, and salmon are all good substitutes.

SOLE DUTY: (with the exception of dark sole) Finely polished, with a mild taste. Skin may be eaten and is, for the most part, rather appetizing.

Broiled, grilled, or fried in a pan.

Cod, flatfish, and haddock whiting are all good substitutes.

STURGEON: White tissue that is dense and exceedingly hard, with a large fat content and a mild taste. Skin isn't something you can eat.

Bake, braise, sear, grill, pocket, sauté, or pan sear are all options. Swordfish and tuna are good substitutes. SWORDFISH: Meaty, thick, hard on the surface, modest fat content, mild taste. Cook, bake, grill, kebab, poach; sauté or mix fry.

Grouper, Halibut, Mahi-Mahi, Red Snapper, Rockfish, Tuna are also good substitutes. FISH BAKED IN AN EASY MANNER

Good for slick-fleshed, dull-fleshed * fish. 1. Place the fish skin side down in a stove glass pan that has been lubricated all around. 2. Apply dissolved margarine or olive oil* to the surface and spritz with lemon juice.

Season with a pinch of sea salt and a pinch of cayenne pepper*.

Bake for 30 minutes at 350°F, or 10 minutes each inch, or until the fish chips when pierced with a fork. 5. If the fish isn't caramelized enough, put it in the oven for 4 minutes, keeping an eye on it.

EASY STUFFED FISH FILLETS BAKED

Use two convenient * fish filets of the same size.

Place one filet on a lubricated stove glass baking dish, brush with lemon juice, and season with salt and pepper.

Cover one of the filets with bread filling and place the second filet on top.

Spread the remaining breadcrumbs evenly on the second fillet. 4. Bake for about 1 hour at 375 degrees, or until the fish falls apart when pierced with a fork.

FISH EASILY BROILED

Broiling oily helpful * fish is usually a good idea.

To aid browning, dry white-fleshed fish may be smeared with softened spread before searing.

Filets or steaks should be cut from larger fish.

Place the fish filets or steaks on a lightly oiled baking sheet or in a lightly oiled baking pan.

The skin side of the split fish is placed down.

Sprinkle with lemon juice, ocean salt, cayenne pepper *, and paprika after brushing with liquefied spread or olive oil *.

Broil for 4 crawls from the oven until the outer layer of the fish is seared, or 10 minutes for each inch of meat, or until the fish pieces when jabbed with a fork. While cooking, give it a squeeze of lemon.

If the fish is thick, turn it over and brush the liquefied spread and spices all over it.

If the fish is small and could self-destruct if turned, cook it for an additional 5-10 minutes on a moderate stove at 350 degrees, or until it drops when jabbed with a fork.

FILLETS OF FISH FRIED IN THE OVEN

Without the fight of frying, baked fish filets have a fresh outside layer and a seared type of singed fish.

2 lbs. olive oil * advantageous *fillets

1 beaten egg or 1 cup soy milk 2 teaspoons salt from the sea

1 cup pieces of Ezekiel bread 4 tbsp. spread (dissolved) lemon juice (two tablespoons)

Using olive oil, grease a broiler glass dish.

Combine the milk and the salt in a blender.

Milk should be used to coat the filets.

Breadcrumbs should be used to coat the chicken.

Arrange in a lubricated baking dish all around.

Mix the softened margarine with the lemon juice, then pour evenly over the breadcrumbs.

Bake at 500°F for 10 minutes per inch of thickness, or until the fish falls apart when pierced with a fork.

PAN FRIED FISH IS EASY TO MAKE.

1 pound * gainful fish, cut into serving pieces 1 teaspoon salt from the sea cayenne pepper, 1/8 teaspoon

a couple of teaspoons of soy milk

14 inch olive oil 1 cup Ezekiel bread crumbs Steps:

Season the fish with salt and pepper before serving.

In a mixing bowl, whisk together the egg and milk.

Cover both sides of the fish with the egg mixture.

Roll in the bread crumbs, making sure they're uniformly distributed.

Fry for 6 to 7 minutes on each side in oil.

When the fish is brown and fresh on both sides, it is ready to eat, and it chips easily when pierced with a fork.

SWORDFISH BAKED AND BROILED

4 fish steaks with blades *

butter (12 cup)

a quarter-cup of lemon juice

4 tsp curry powder (optional)

12 tsp. garlic salt

12 teaspoon paprika 1 tablespoon margarine, softened lemon juice, 1 tbsp

14 teaspoon paprika 14 teaspoon parsley (optional)

Place the steaks in foil baskets that are hidden.

Melt the spread and stir in the next four ingredients.

Pour the sauce over the steaks.

Wrap the steaks in foil and tuck them in securely.

Preheat oven to 450°F and bake for 30 minutes.

Combine the spread and lemon juice in a mixing bowl.

Take the fish out of the oven.

Remove the foil baskets from the oven.

Brush the lemon butter over top.

Paprika and parsley are sprinkled over top.

Broil for about 2 minutes, or until golden brown. 1 cup ground horseradish * 1 slashed onion * 2 tablespoons margarine BAKED HALIBUT lbs. halibut filets 1/3 cup liquid

Place all of the ingredients in a baking dish.

Preheat the oven to 350°F and bake for 20 minutes, or until the fish pieces are flaky when pierced with a fork. lb. roost filets of BAKED PERCH

1 tablespoon Ezekiel breadcrumbs, dry 1 tablespoon Mozzarella cheese, grated paprika (1 tablespoon)

1 tsp basil powder 1 tablespoon softened spread * 1/8 teaspoon ginger Steps:

Butter the filets before serving.

Combine the bread, cheddar cheese, paprika, basil, and ginger in a mixing bowl.

Toss the fish in the scrap mixture and roll it around.

Place the fish in a glass baking dish that has been lubricated.

Bake for 10 minutes at 450 degrees, uncovered, or until the fish pieces are flaky when pierced with a fork.

PIKE BAKED

14 cup melted butter 4 garlic cloves squashed

12 cup cut yam * 12 cup diced Spanish onions * 1 12 pound deboned finely cleaved pike filets

12 CUP SELECTED SELECTED SELECTED SELECTED SELECTED SEL

12 tablespoon oats, rolled

14 cup mozzarella cheese, 14 cup mozzarella cheese, 14 cup mozzarella cheese, 14 cup mozzarella cheese, 14 cup mozzarella cheese, 14 cup mozzarella cheese, 14 Combine the spread, garlic, potato, onion, and fish in a mixing bowl.

Combine flour, oats, and cheese in a mixing bowl.

Fill an ovenproof dish halfway with the potato mixture.

Top with the flour mixture and a sprinkling of the remaining cheese.

Preheat oven to 400°F and bake for 25 minutes, or until golden brown. RED SNAPPER BAKED 3 pound filets of red snapper

1 garlic clove, minced 4 tablespoons olive oil * 1 tablespoon lemon juice 1 teaspoon sea salt 14 teaspoon cayenne pepper

12 teaspoon sugar with an earthy color 2 hacked onions * 4 cleaved celery stalks * tablespoons slashed parsley * 14 teaspoon squashed dried thyme 1 massive cove leaf

2 cups stewed tomatoes, hacked

1 tsp. parsley

12 cup scallion greens, cleaved * liquefied spread soy sauce, 3 tblsp

2 tblsp pineapple juice (optional) 1 teaspoon of soy sauce

sugar 1 tbsp

14 cup onions * 1 teaspoon new ground ginger 4 whole garlic cloves

1 garlic clove * 1/8 teaspoon cayenne pepper

12 pound filets of yellowtail Steps:

To make the marinade, combine all of the ingredients (except the fish) in a mixing bowl.

Toss in the fish. 1–2 hours in the marinade Turn the wheel every now and then. 3. Oil the barbecue or oven dish and cook, or sear, the fish for about 5 minutes on one side, then turn and cook for another 5 minutes on the other side, or until a fish drops when pierced with a fork.

COD FILETS WITH SPINACH *

12 cup sherry for cooking

2/3 cup crumbled mozzarella cheese a third of a cup of Ezekiel breadcrumbs

12 tblsp. melted butter

12 tblsp parsley * 12 tblsp lemon, cut

3 garlic cloves, squashed * 3 tablespoons olive oil

12 teaspoon garlic salt 6 cups coarse spinach * leaves

lemon juice (two teaspoons)

Place the cod in a baking dish and bake it (assuming any skin stays on the cod, place the cod skin side down).

Over the fish, pour the sherry.

Mix together the cheddar and breadcrumbs, then sprinkle them over the cod.

Spread taps of spread over the fish's highest point.

Broil for 15 minutes or until the fish turns hazy or breaks apart when pierced with a fork.

If the fish isn't done after 15 minutes, lower the stove temperature to 350 degrees and cook for another 5-10 minutes.

Serve with a parsley garnish.

Serve on a spinach bed.

Serve with lemon slices as a garnish.

1 minute after heating the oil, fry the garlic.

Mix in the spinach over high heat until it has shriveled. Don't wilt too much.

Return the spinach to the pan after draining the excess water.

Warm again with a pinch of salt and a squeeze of lemon.

SWORDFISH ON THE GRILL

a quarter-cup of soy sauce

14 cup pineapple, unsweetened * 14 cup sherry tablespoon brown sugar

12 teaspoon ginger * 1 garlic clove minced teaspoons pineapple

4 swordfish steaks * juice

Steps: In a glass bowl, combine the marinade ingredients and pour over the steaks. Alternatively, pour it into a baggie and submerge the fish completely in the marinade.

In the refrigerator, marinate for 1 to 2 hours. To completely marinate all of the fish's surfaces, turn or throw the fish a few times. 3. Take the swordfish out of the pack (or the bowl).

4. Brush the grill with oil. Place the fish on the grill and cook it for 4 to 5 minutes on each side over high heat. Avoid overcooking the swordfish because it dries out quickly. YELLOWTAIL GRILLED

4 filets of yellowtail stew powder (four tablespoons) 4 teaspoons salt from the sea

* Olive oil * 1 teaspoon cayenne pepper

12 tablespoons margarine liquefied and enough soy milk to make 12 gallon milk 12 cup mozzarella cheese that has been ruined

14 cup small shrimp

Cut the fish into serving pieces and layer them in a lubed glass baking dish in a single layer.

Soften the spread in a pan, then add the flour and cook until it's all gone.

bubbly.

Season with salt, mustard, dill, and cayenne pepper.

Remove from the heat and gradually stir in the cream. Return to a high heat setting and stir until the mixture is thick.

1 cup cheddar cheese should be mixed in with the shrimp.

Pour the sauce over the fish and top with the remaining cheese.

Preheat the oven to 400°F and bake for 20 minutes, or until the fish pieces are flaky when pierced with a fork.

RED SNAPPER RED SNAPPER RED SNAPPER

12 pound filets of snapper * 14 cup spelt flour

butter tblsp

12 cup hacked red pepper * 2/3 cup cleaved celery 12 cup slashed onion

tomato sauce (cups)

12 teaspoon powdered bean stew 1 12 tblsp lemon juice 1 cove leaf 1 garlic clove, minced

12 tsp sodium

* Parsley* 1/8 teaspoon cayenne pepper

Coat the snapper in flour and place it in a baking dish.

Bake for 45 minutes at 350 degrees, or until the fish falls apart when pierced with a fork. Every 15 minutes, season with salt and pepper.

In a skillet, melt the margarine.

Cook for 10 minutes with the onion, celery, and pepper.

Combine the tomatoes, stew powder, lemon juice, narrows leaf, garlic, salt, and pepper in a large mixing bowl. Cook for an additional 10 minutes.

Blend the vegetables in a blender until they become a smooth sauce.

Over the fish, pour the sauce.

Parsley can be added as a finishing touch. LEMON SOUR SOLE * 1 tablespoon lemon juice 1 pound sole filets dissolved 2 tbsp

margarine 2 tbsp. spelt flour, 3 tbsp 1 gallon soy milk

paprika, 1/8 tsp 1 tablespoon butter + 1 egg yolk lemon juice, 3 tablespoons cup Paprika * parsley * parsley * parsley * parsley * parsley * par

Place the filets in a stove glass dish with the skin side down.

Lemon juice, if desired.

Each filet should be rolled up tightly.

Using a toothpick, secure the pieces together.

Using liquefied butter as a brush, coat the entire surface.

Bake for 20 minutes at 350°F, or until the fish falls apart when pierced with a fork.

In a saucepan, melt the butter.

To make a paste, add in the flour.

To make the sauce, gradually pour in milk.

Once that's done, add the rest of the ingredients and stir until everything is well combined.

Remove the toothpicks after the fish is fully cooked.

Hollandaise Sauce should be served on the side.

Add parsley and paprika to the top. 3 2 inch thick cuts onion * STEAMED SEA BASS tablespoons olive oil

Ocean bass, 1 pound

* 12 cup cut scallion with chives * 12 cup cleaved cilantro * 1 little stripped daintily cut gingerroot arugula Steps:

Fill a large pot halfway with olive oil and set aside.

On the oiled bottom, place the onions.

Toss the onions with the bass and serve.

On top of the fish, sprinkle the ginger, scallions, and cilantro. If you want more, just ask.

1 12 inch of water should be in the pot.

Cover the pot and steam the fish until it flakes when a fork is poked through it.

If needed, add more water.

Parsley can be added as a finishing touch. FISH TENDERS is a title given to a group of people who work in the fishing industry. 14 + teaspoon cayenne pepper 1 cup spelt 12 teaspoon sea salt

title fish fillets * 1 12 pound pepper

soy milk, egg tablespoons

lemon juice, 1 tbsp

14 teaspoon sea salt 14 teaspoon cayenne pepper * 14 teaspoon chili powder 1 12 cup Ezekiel breadcrumbs 14 teaspoon sea salt 14 teaspoon cayenne pepper

12 tbsp oil (canola) Steps:

Mix the flour, salt, and pepper together in a mixing bowl.

The fish should be cut into 4 x 12 inch tender pieces.

Fish should be dredged in flour.

Combine the egg, lemon juice, and milk in a mixing bowl and whisk to combine.

Breadcrumbs, salt, pepper, and chili powder should be combined in a separate bowl.

Coat the fish in the egg mixture, then breadcrumbs.

Place the fish on the baking sheet after brushing it with canola oil.

Preheat the oven to 425°F and bake the fish for about 10 minutes, or until it flakes easily when poked with a fork.

Chapter 8 Desserts Bars and Cookies

Chapter 7

PRUNE BAR, APRICOT, DATE, FIG

eggs (three)

12 CUP SUGAR 12 CUP SUGAR (12 CUP SUGAR) 12 CUP SUGAR (12 CUP 1 tsp vanilla, 1 cup spelt flour, 1 tsp baking powder

1 cup chopped walnuts * 14 teaspoon cloves teaspoon cinnamon cups chopped dates, apricot, figs *, and prunes *

eggs (three)

sugar, 12 cup

a quarter cup of honey and a teaspoon of vanilla extract

Combine the flour and 14 cup sugar in a mixing bowl. Then, using a pastry blender, chop the butter into the mixture until coarse crumbs form.

In a lightly greased 13 x 9-inch baking pan, press the crust in the bottom. 3. Cook for 15 minutes at 350°F.

4. Decorate the crust with figs, walnuts, and chocolate chips. 5. Lightly whisk the eggs, then gradually add the 12 cup sugar, honey, and vanilla extract until well combined.

Bake for another 20-30 minutes, or until the filling is firm around the edges and slightly soft in the middle.

Allow to cool completely before slicing into bars.

Puddings and cakes

SAUCE WITH BLUE CHERRY

12 tbsp. tapioca in a minute

12 cup black cherry juice * 14 cup cold water 12 teaspoon

ice cream with cinnamon soy

Steps: Combine the tapioca, cherry juice, and cinnamon in a bowl and mix well. Reheat, stirring constantly, until the sauce has thickened.

Over ice cream is a great way to serve this dish. CAKE MADE WITH CARROT

sugar, cup

Canola oil (112 cup)

2 cups beaten eggs 4 eggs

flour made with spelt

baking powder, 4 tablespoons 12 tsp. bicarbonate 2 tsp cinnamon, 1 tsp salt

* 1 cup chopped walnuts * 2 cups shredded carrots * 8 oz. crushed drained pineapple

6 TBS BUTTER (SOFT) 14 cup (2 14)

sugar granules 12 tsp vanilla 1 egg

14 cup icing sugar (powdered)

Milk made from soy

To make the sugar and oil frothy, cream them together until light and fluffy.

In a separate bowl, whisk together the eggs until well combined.

Combine flour and spices in a mixing bowl. Combine all of the ingredients in a mixing bowl and cream them together until smooth. Avoid overmixing the ingredients.

Carrots, pineapple, and walnuts should all be mixed together. Toss into the mix. Don't overmix this time, either.

Fill a greased 13x9x2 inch baking pan halfway with the batter.

Preheat oven to 350°F and bake for 55–65 minutes, or until toothpick inserted in middle comes out clean.

6 tblsp. butter, creamed together till light and fluffy

Half of the powdered sugar should be added gradually and well beaten.

In a separate bowl, whisk together the egg and the vanilla extract.

Pour in the rest of the sugar. To make the frosting easier to spread, add milk if required. PUDDING CAKE WITH CHERRY

sugar (1 cup)

1 cup flour oats 1 tsp bicarbonate

cinnamon (1 teaspoon) salt, 1/8 teaspoon

12 c. walnuts, chopped

1 egg, whisked

* 1 tablespoon melted butter * 14.5 oz. can drained, saving liquid unsweetened red cherries 1 cup cherry juice + 1 cup water 2 tblsp. tapioca in a minute

sugar, 12 cup

14 cup butter

1 cup sugar, flour, baking soda, cinnamon, salt, and nuts should be mixed together.

In a medium mixing bowl, beat the egg with the cherries and butter.

In a mixing bowl, combine the flour and cherry mixture.

Fill a 9 x 12 inch baking dish halfway with the batter.

Cook for 40 minutes at 350°F.

Cook over medium heat, stirring regularly, until the cherry water, tapioca, salt, and 12 cup sugar have thickened. 1 tbsp. butter, stirred in until melted

To serve, cut the cake into squares and pour the sauce on top. CHERRY PUDDING WITH CHOCOLATE 14 cup soy milk 3 oz rice cream cheese

12 cup soy milk, 8 oz. instant chocolate pudding, 2 teaspoons tapioca starch a third of a cup of black cherry juice (optional)

1 14.5 oz. can red sour pitted cherries, drained

Steps: In a low-powered blender, combine cream cheese and milk until smooth.

Combine the remaining milk and pudding milk in a mixing bowl. 1 to 2 minutes of mixing time, or until smooth.

In a saucepan, thicken the tapioca with the cherry juice.

Cook for 1 minute with the cherries in the sauce. Take the pan off the heat and add the sugar.

Spoon pudding and cherries into dessert dishes in that order, starting with the pudding and ending with the cherries.

Chill.

CAKE WITH PINEAPPLE ON TOP

unsweetened pineapple slices, halved 8 oz. can drained (reserve the juice) 4 halved maraschino cherries * 1 tbsp. butter

12 CUP SUGAR (BROWN)

12 c. butter (softened)

sugar, 34 cup 1 ovary

12 tsp vanilla extract

34 teaspoons baking powder 12 cup spelt flour

2/3 cup reserved juice plus 2/3 cup water

Streusels and pies are two of the most popular dishes in Germany.

SHELLS FOR PASTRY

PIE SHELL WITH A SINGLE CRUST

12 teaspoon iodized salt 1/8 cup spelt flour Crisco (about 1/3 cup)

3–4 tbsp. chilled water

SHELL WITH DOUBLE CRUST

spelt flour (14 cups) 1 tsp. salt (iodized) Crisco 2/3 cup cold water, 1/3-1/2 cup

Combine the flour and salt in a large mixing bowl.

Cut the fat into the dry ingredients until pea-sized.

Cut in with a fork until the dry ingredients are dampened. To make a smooth ball, add a pinch of water if necessary.

Using a floured pastry cloth, roll the dough into a ball(s).

From the center outward, roll the dough.

Fold it in half and place it in the pie plate when it's flat and large enough.

Fill the pastry with your favorite filling and top with the second pastry, fluted edges.

Follow the pie's instructions for baking. PASTRY SHELL THAT HAS BEEN BAKED

Prepare a Single Crust Pie Shell and place a second pie plate on top of it to keep it from shrinking while baking, or prick the bottom and sides with a fork.

Cook for 10 to 12 minutes, or until golden brown, at 450 degrees.

1 tablespoon finely chopped walnuts NUTTY PIE SHELL Single-Crust Shell

Shell with 2 Crusts

a third of a cup of walnuts, finely chopped

Prepare the pie shells as directed, but before adding the water, add the nuts. GUAVA PIE consists of unbaked pastry shells with acceptable fillings.

oat flour, 2 tbsp sugar, 2/3 cup

salt, 1/8 teaspoon

3 tablespoons butter, cut into pieces * cup seeded and sliced guavas * 4 teaspoons pineapple juice

Fill a pie pan halfway with pastry shells and set aside.

Combine flour, sugar, and salt in a large mixing bowl.

Mound the guavas in the center of the pie pan.

Over the guavas, sprinkle the flour mixture evenly.

Add the pineapple juice and mix well. Using butter as a dot

The second pastry shell should be placed on top of the filling to protect it. To allow steam to escape, make several slashes in the top.

Bake for 10 minutes at 450 degrees Fahrenheit, then reduce to 350 degrees Fahrenheit for another 30 to 40 minutes.

2 unbaked pastry shells of acceptable ingredients for a mango pie

12 teaspoon cinnamon 14 teaspoon ginger * 1 cup sugar, tablespoons oat flour

1 tablespoon lemon juice * cup sliced ripe mango 1 to 2 tbsp soy milk

Step 1: Roll out the puff pastry and line the bottom of a pie pan.

Sugar, flour, cinnamon, and ginger should all be mixed together.

Place a layer of sliced mangoes in the bottom of the pastry shell, then sprinkle them with the sugar mixture. Continue layering the mangoes and spices alternately until all of the mangoes have been used.

After that, squeeze some lemon juice over the filling before covering it with the top pastry. To let steam out, make several slashes in the top.

Bake for 10 minutes at 425 degrees Fahrenheit, then reduce to 350 degrees Fahrenheit for another 30 to 40 minutes.

PIZZA WITH PLUMS

1 acceptable ingredients unbaked pastry shell

4 cup fresh plums, pitted and sliced

14 teaspoon salt 14 teaspoon cinnamon 12 cup sugar 14 cup spelt flour

* 1 tsp pineapple juice

sugar, 12 cup

12 teaspoon cinnamon 14 cup spelt flour

14 tsp allspice powder butter, 3 tablespoons

Fill the pastry shell with a mixture of plums, sugar, flour, salt, cinnamon, and pineapple juice.

In a large mixing bowl, combine the remaining sugar, flour, cinnamon, and allspice, and cut in the butter until it crumbles. Toss the plums with a pinch of salt and pepper.

Cook for 50-60 minutes at 375°F. To prevent the crust from overbrowning, cover the edges with foil during the last 20 minutes.

POTATO PUDDING WITH SUGAR

12 cup sweet potatoes* 3 12 cup sweet potatoes

a cup of soy milk (14 to 12 oz.)

butter (12 cup) 3 cup sugar 4 eggs

34 cup sugar (brown) baking powder, 2 tsp cinnamon (1 teaspoon)

12 tsp ginger (optional) cloves (1/8 teaspoon)

2Mix in the margarine until a crumbly consistency is achieved.

Sprinkle the plums with water and cinnamon in an 8x8 inch baking dish. Spread streusel on top.

Bake for 30 minutes at 375°F, or until the top is lightly browned. HYPERLINK HYPERLINK HYPERLINK HYPERLINK HYPERLINK HYPER

M.D. Steven Weissberg and Joseph Christiano Your Bloodtype Holds the Key. Person Nutrition in the United States of America, Florida, 1999

Joseph Christiano You, Your Bloodtype, and Your Bodytype Siloam Press, Inc., in Florida, published the book in the year 2000.

Eat Right For Your Type, P. D'Adamo, P. D'Adamo, P. D'Adamo, P. D'A Putnam, 1996, New York. P. D'Adamo, P. D'Adamo, P. d'Adamo, P. d'Adamo, P Berkley, 1999, New York. JOE

CPSIA information can be obtained
at www.ICGtesting.com
Printed in the USA
LVHW020805060422
715456LV00007B/275